ANTONIUS STRADIVARIUS

39

SYMPHONIA BOOKS

A SERIES OF CONTRIBUTIONS TO THE HISTORY OF MUSIC

ANTONIUS STRADIVARIUS

TRANSLATED FROM THE DUTCH BY W. A. G. DOYLE-DAVIDSON
PROFESSOR OF ENGLISH IN THE UNIVERSITY OF NIJMEGEN

THE CONTINENTAL BOOK COMPANY A. B., STOCKHOLM

ANTONIUS STRADIVARIUS

BY

DIRK J. BALFOORT

ASSISTANT DIRECTOR OF THE MUNICIPAL MUSEUM AT THE HAGUE

THE CONTINENTAL BOOK COMPANY A. B., STOCKHOLM

TOWARDS the end of the sixteenth century there was a reaction against the polyphonic music of the contrapuntists who for some four centuries had dominated music. Music had for far too long turned but one of its facets to the world. Art cannot live, however, without being constantly renewed, and when one genre has reached full maturity the need inevitably arises to emphasise some other aspect. This was the case here. The Renaissance, which for a whole century had brought its revolutionary forces to bear in other directions, at last made its influence felt in the sphere of music too; man stepped out from the group as an individual. Thus in Florence, where the foundations had been laid for the new views and ideas, we see the rise of the so-called monodic style, which above all demanded solos. Music was placed at the service of drama and recitation; a solo voice and accompanying musical instruments followed the text closely. Instruments, which had so far been almost exclusively restricted to accompanying, found themselves called upon to perform solo work. As the melodic element now naturally came very much to the fore, it is easy to understand that the violin, the melody instrument *par excellence*, was destined thenceforward to play an important rôle.

Evolved in the course of the 16th century from the mediæval fiddle, it had not at first been held in any great esteem. Only the troubadours and the wandering minstrels had used it to play jolly tunes and to accompany dances. Now, however, that it began to fill a certain want, it soon became the centre of attraction. Indeed, its standing increased to such an extent that after a certain length of time it came to be looked upon as the Queen of musical instruments. At first, however, neither its form nor its tone were very regal; it still bore too clearly the traces of the poverty in which it

I

had been brought up. But this was soon to change. Our lute makers, who hitherto had paid but scant attention to the minstrel's fiddle, now became interested in this instrument and vied with one another in making both the tone and form of the violin worthy of the royal dignity to which it had been called. Particularly in Italy, the home of *bel canto*, where the climatic conditions were so favourable for the making of violins, artists of the highest skill and genius applied their talents to improving the violin; in their hands violin making reached a height unequalled anywhere else in the world. The concepts 'violin' and 'Italy' are thus inseparably connected. In no other country in the world has any one been able to make violins which in beauty of tone and form can compare with the creations of a Maggini at Brescia or of one of the famous representatives of the school of Cremona.

Cremona! What a venerable halo does this insignificant little town in the plain of the Po bear for every violin enthusiast! The mere mention of the name is sufficient to carry him in thought to the place where such men as the Amatis, Guarnerius and Stradivarius wrought their miracles.

That it was just in Cremona that the art of violin making should have developed to such an unprecedented height is in no small part due to a certain Andreas Amati, who had settled there as a violin maker in the latter half of the 16th century. It was he who became the ancestor of the famous Amati family of violin makers. Its chief representative, Nicolas, was in his turn the teacher of various other great violin makers, including our Antonius Stradivarius, who alone would undoubtedly have made the name of Cremona famous. In him we salute the greatest violin maker of all time, who was occasionally equalled but never excelled by his compatriot and contemporary, Joseph Guarnerius del Gesù.

The name Stradivarius was known long before the 17th century. Its first bearer was probably a customs official; at least the word *stradiere*—of which Stradivari seems to be the Lombardic form— has this meaning. The name is met with both in the Lombardic form 'Antonio Stradivari' and in the Latin form 'Antonius Stradivarius'.

Hill, from whose book I have derived much information, assumes that Stradivarius was born in 1644 as the son of Allessandro Stradivari and Anna Moroni, to whom Allessandro was married at Cremona

2

on 30 August 1622. His father's name, as appears from a deed of sale of Antonio's house drawn up in 1680, was certainly Allessandro, but this Allessandro was not married to Anna Morini.

MEDALLION OF STRADIVARIUS BY FRANCESCO GIALDISI

In the years 1628 and 1629 Cremona was ravaged by a terrible famine and in 1630 by the plague, which caused dire havoc among the population. Those days saw a veritable exodus from the perishing city and within a few months Cremona was almost completely deserted. As the city registers make no mention of the children

3

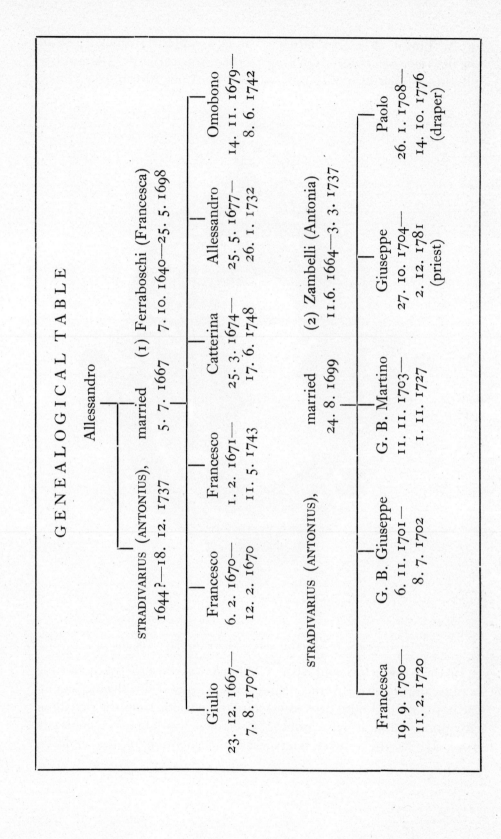

GENEALOGICAL TABLE

Allessandro

STRADIVARIUS (ANTONIUS),   married   (1) Ferraboschi (Francesca)
1644?—18. 12. 1737   5. 7. 1667   7. 10. 1640—25. 5. 1698

Giulio   Francesco   Francesco   Catterina   Allessandro   Omobono
23. 12. 1667—   6. 2. 1670—   1. 2. 1671—   25. 3. 1674—   25. 5. 1677—   14. 11. 1679—
7. 8. 1707   12. 2. 1670   11. 5. 1743   17. 6. 1748   26. 1. 1732   8. 6. 1742

STRADIVARIUS (ANTONIUS),   married   (2) Zambelli (Antonia)
                             24. 8. 1699   11.6. 1664—3. 3. 1737

Francesca   G. B. Giuseppe   G. B. Martino   Giuseppe   Paolo
19. 9. 1700—   6. 11. 1701 —   11. 11. 1703—   27. 10. 1704—   26. 1. 1708—
11. 2. 1720   8. 7. 1702   1. 11. 1727   2. 12. 1781   14. 10. 1776
                                                                  (priest)   (draper)

born to him after 1628, though they do mention the three born of this marriage in 1623, 1626 and 1628 respectively, Hill concludes that Allessandro also fled the city on that occasion. From the Registers of Deaths of the city of Cremona it appears, however, that the father of these children had died of the plague in 1630. Antonio's father must therefore have been a different Allessandro, but who this was we do not know. Neither his domicile or his profession, his wife's name or Antonio's birth certificate are known, so that we are left in the dark as regards both the date and the place of Antonio's birth.

For a time it was hoped that the census registers, which were regularly brought up to date by the priests of the various parishes, would have shed some light at least on the date of Antonio's birth, but these registers proved to contain so many contradictions that they cannot possibly be looked upon as reliable sources of information. Thus Stradivarius is recorded as being 28 years of age in 1668, 22 in 1669, 25 in 1672, 28 in 1675 and 30 in 1676, but as being 29 again in both 1677 and 1678. Then there is an equally unreliable document relating to his confirmation in the year 1681, in which his age is given as 32.

Hill's conviction that Stradivarius was born in 1644 is founded simply on the fact that towards the end of his life on some of his labels, besides the year in which the instrument was made, he also mentions his age. On the printed label of a violin of the year 1735, for instance, he has added in ink "d'anni 91". All these data lead back to the year 1644, and for Hill this solved the problem. Now, however, Bacchetta, in his little book on Stradivarius, states that Hill has allowed himself to be misled by these additions, for they were inserted not by Stradivarius himself, but partly by his son Omobono and partly by a later owner of these instruments, Count Cozio di Salabue. Bacchetta's arguments are for the rest far from convincing. The proof that he brings forward to show that Stradivarius was born at the end of 1648 or the beginning of 1649 is also highly questionable. Here he appeals to the so-called "Stati d'anime", but we have seen what value is to be attributed to official documents in those days. As long as no better arguments can be advanced in favour of another year of birth, it is better to stick to Hill's conclusion that Stradivarius was born in 1644.

Neither do we know how Antonius came to choose the profession

5

of violin maker or in what year he was apprenticed at Cremona to Nicolas Amati. An impenetrable veil, indeed, lies over the whole of his youth. The oldest document that we possess about him is a violin with a label on which can be read "Antonius Stradivarius Cremonensis Alumnus Nicolaii Amati Faciebat Anno 1666". From this it would therefore appear not only that Antonius had already made violins by 1666 but also that he had been a pupil of Nicolas Amati. For us this label is of the greatest value because neither on his labels of later date nor in any other manner did Stradivarius ever again mention that Amati had been his master.

That he had turned to Amati will be readily understood, for of all violin makers in Italy Nicolas Amati was in those days the most highly esteemed, not only as an artist but also as a teacher.

He was a son of Girolamo Amati, the youngest son of that Andreas Amati who, as we have seen, was the founder of the family.

There are, however, other reasons why Andreas is a very important figure in the history of violin making: not only was it, as we have already seen, thanks to him and his followers that Cremona had become the most important centre of violin making in Italy, but he was also the creator of a model of violin the broad lines of which were followed by most of the members of his family and which has become characteristic of Amati instruments in general: a small, fairly high-arched model with a very fine, it is true, yet on the whole thin tone.

At first he built according to tradition on the viol models, and it was only gradually that Andreas came to adopt the violin shape. His varnish also changed in the course of time; originally he used a blackish red but later a dark yellow and pale brown varnish, which unfortunately has been laid on somewhat too thickly.

His work fell after him into good hands, in the persons of his sons Antonio (c. 1555 till after 1640) and Girolamo (c. 1556 to 1630) who had inherited their father's talent. The greatest artist in the family, however, was to be the tenth of Girolamo's fourteen children, our Nicolas Amati (1596–1684). In him we find the perfect artist. With his artistic gifts he combined also a great love of study, and the fruits of this earned him immortal fame in the history of violin making.

Nicolas began as an apprentice to his father, whose example he followed faithfully until 1625, after which his own personality

VIOLIN BY ANDREAS AMATI, 1574

gradually came to the fore and after many years of hard work he created his "great Amati model", which made his name. The curve and the thickness of the front of the body, or soundboard, are less than in his father's instruments and finer than in those of any of his predecessors, the *ff* or sound-holes are nobler in shape, the corners stand out conspicuously, the scroll is usually small but elegant, the wood unerringly selected, and the varnish, from pale yellow to reddish gold, is elastic and warm. These instruments are perfect works of art, although their tone, alas, is not great in volume.

It was inevitable that under the guidance of such an artist our Antonio, with his outstanding gifts, would make great progress. And in the first steps that he took on the path which was to lead him to world fame he allowed himself to be guided entirely by Nicolas Amati.

No details are known about Stradivarius' apprentice years, but century-old traditions which have been preserved down to the present day in violin-making circles enable us to form some idea of these first steps of his in the art of violin making.

As is still the custom to-day, those wishing to learn the art of making violins were formerly also apprenticed at a very early age to a master violin maker, under whose guidance they generally completed their whole apprenticeship. The sole requirement imposed, at least at the present day, regarding their general education, is that they should have successfully passed though the elementary school. The master is entirely indifferent to their further capacities and lacunae; he limits himself to teaching them to make violins. The acquisition of skill in the craft is the sole object aimed at. Just as a joiner's apprentice learns how to make a cupboard, so the future maker of violins learns everything he needs to know in order to be able to produce a violin; the tone of the instrument is quite a secondary matter. If a violin should happen to have a good tone, so much the better; the main thing however, is the craftsmanship-to learn to carve a scroll, to curve the soundboard and back, to insert the ribs, and so on. Not a single text-book is consulted; after having successfully completed his years of service, the apprentice knows as little about the science of acoustics, for instance, as his master, who may nevertheless be an excellent violin maker. All knowledge is acquired by practice and experiment, and after his apprenticeship, which as a rule lasts three years, the pupil, now promoted to master,

8

VIOLIN BY NICOLAS AMATI

continues along this road, except that now he will also devote full attention to the tone of the instrument, at least if he aspires to become an artist in his craft. Many a violin maker has in this manner risen to great heights without ever having concerned himself with scientific books dealing with his subject.

There are of course exceptions. Some of them have indeed attempted to obtain their knowledge of the 'secrets' of violin making from heavy, learned tomes, but as a rule such men are more distinguished by their knowledge than by their practical ability. Those who have really heard the call seek for themselves, continually experimenting, till at last they evolve a theory of their own based solely upon empirical knowledge.

This, it seems to me, must more or less have been the case with Stradivarius. Apprenticed to Amati as a boy of 12 or 14, equipped with a minimum of general knowledge, during his whole life he allowed himself to be guided by his own genius, which, aided by his industrious and persevering spirit and his unfailing delight in experiment, ultimately succeeded in solving brilliantly every problem that presented itself.

He began to make violins under his own name in the years 1660–1665, as we know from the labels on violins of this period. We need not, however, conclude from this that he had left Amati's workshop and had set up on his own; it only proves that he was free to make instruments under his own name if he so desired. It would seem, however, that at that time this desire rarely arose in him, for very few instruments dating from this period are known that bear his own label.

The reason why Stradivarius had at that time not yet set up on his own is in part, at least, probably to be sought in a natural desire on the part of Amati to keep his talented pupil with him as long as possible. On the other hand, Stradivarius will also have realised the advantage of this, for it goes without saying that important commissions would sooner be given to a man of Amati's reputation than to a violin maker whose name was still practically unknown beyond the gates of his native city.

It is also obvious that when he made his first violins Stradivarius was still entirely under the influence of Amati and that it was only gradually that he came to strike out on a path of his own.

He did not, as was formerly too readily assumed, appear suddenly as a brilliant meteor in the firmament. On the contrary, he only developed very slowly and the great examples of the art of his later period were the results of a very deep and lengthy, laborious and persevering study.

In his early instruments, in which he did his best to approach as nearly as possible to those of Amati, but few signs can be discerned of the great genius that was later to come to such full maturity. During his first years he was certainly not conspicuous amongst his fellow-pupils. This is not surprising if we remember that in those days men like Andreas Guarnerius, Giovanni Battista Rogeri, Francesco Ruger and Amati's own son Jerome—all of whom were subsequently to gain great reputations—were apprenticed to Amati at the same time as Stradivarius. It was in this environment that Stradivarius passed the first thirty years of his life.

When Nicolas became an old man, he left a good deal of the work to his pupils. Remarkably enough, however, though the instruments of that period reveal traces of the work of Guarnerius, Rogeri or Ruger, the typical qualities that even at that time already characterised the work of Stradivarius are to be sought for in them in vain. Neither do we know exactly what Stradivarius' work was at that time. It is assumed that his task will have been principally the varnishing and the assembling of the parts and supervision of the work in general.

Or perhaps Stradivarius worked together with Jerome, in which case the personal character of neither of them would be distinguishable. In any case it is a fact that the beautifully finished violins that date from the year in which Amati died were the work either of Jerome alone or of Jerome and Stradivarius together.

In the meantime, in the year 1667, Stradivarius had married the 27-year-old Francesca Ferabosca, the widow of a certain Giovanni Giacomo Capra, the marriage being solemnised on 4 July of that year in the Church of St. Agatha at Cremona. The young couple established themselves in the 'Casa del Pescatore', in which they lived until 1680.

Of this marriage six children were born, of whom the second, Francesco, died six days after birth (see Genealogical Table on p. 4). Two sons also became violin makers, namely, Francesco (b. 1671) and Omobono (b. 1679). We shall return to them later.

Most biographers of Stradivarius divide his life into periods, usually praising one period inordinately at the expense of another.

THE "HELLIER" STRADIVARIUS, 1679

To a certain extent this is misleading, for a man of the remarkable talents of a Stradivarius would never have been able to allow himself to be bound within strictly defined limits.

This division into periods is based on the three different models he designed, although after the creation of each new model he still continued to make the earlier ones. It would therefore be a great mistake to assume that a division into periods implies that in a certain period only one particular model was produced. It is therefore better to abandon altogether this division of Stradivarius' life into definite periods.

As regards the appreciation of these periods, in each were produced instruments that must be counted among his greatest works of art. During the whole of his life Stradivarius worked very unequally, for in all periods we find, side by side with unsurpassable masterpieces, instruments of inferior quality. The most one can say is that, while pressing forwards, he always tried to profit by experience, thus avoiding as far as possible the mistakes he had made earlier.

His unremitting experimentation—somewhat more intense before 1700 than after this date—resulted in this ideas turning out sometimes well, sometimes less happily, but never so badly that one can speak of poor workmanship. Even the less successful specimens of his skill never belied his genius.

It is a remarkable fact, characteristic of Stradivarius' inquiring mind, that he did not at once adopt Amati's 'Great Model' as his exemplar. He was apparently not convinced that therein lay the cause of the greater volume of sound produced by these violins. It is also possible, however, that the demand for instruments with the clear though thinner tone of the small model was the reason for his long retention of this smaller type.

The instruments Stradivarius made before 1684 are stronger and more solidly made than those of his former master. With Nicolas Amati everything is elegant and fine; look at the delicate ribs and the slender corners, the gracefully carved scroll and the elegant sound-holes of the Amati violins and compare these with the Stradivarius violins of the same period. In the latter the corners are much shorter and blunter, the sound-holes—which as a rule are closer to each other than in Amati's instruments—are more angular.

A typical example of Stradivarius' method at that time is the so-called "Hellier" violin of the year 1679. It is true that the fine symmetrically carved scroll and the delicately finished sound-holes far excel all other work of the same period, but the whole construction nevertheless makes a too heavy and solid, one might almost say too clumsy, impression. It cannot be denied, however, that this heaviness is almost neutralised by the inlaid tendril motive with which the instrument is delicately adorned (see illustration on p. 12).

As far as can be ascertained, Stradivarius never applied such decoration to his instruments before 1677. The idea was by no means original. The old lute makers of the 16th century were already in the habit of embellishing their instruments with inlaid work or painting, but in the course of the 17th century this custom disappeared entirely, although the finger-board, string-holder, pegs and bridge were still occasionally ornamented.

That in a few instruments Stradivarius spent his valuable time in this long and tedious work must have been due to the desires of his clients. There is no doubt that the beautifully executed figures, flowers, fruits and arabesques, sometimes painted, sometimes inlaid with ebony and ivory, must have greatly pleased the noble gentlemen for whom such instruments were intended.

Hill mentions a total of 8 violins, one viola and a violoncello decorated in this manner, but that there must have been more he concludes from the fact that he once came across an old English violin of poor quality that had a beautifully inlaid soundboard by Stradivarius.

We have already pointed out the difference between Stradivarius' and Amati's methods. There were also, however, many points of similarity, such as the yellow colour of the varnish—which in the course of time, however, Stradivarius laid on in increasingly darker tints—and the method in which the soundboard and back are cut

CROSS SECTION OF TREE TRUNK   CROSS SECTION OF TREE TRUNK
CUT RADIALLY OR 'QUARTERED'   CUT ALONG PARALLEL PLANES

from the tree trunk. In both cases the trunk is cut in the length, but in the first case (see figure above) the cross section of the piece cut out is the sector of a circle. To obtain this the trunk is cut radially, or quartered, to show the grain to advantage. In the second case (see figure above) the trunk is cut along two parallel planes. The cross section of the plank thus cut out is here limited by two parallel lines and the sections of the circumference lying between them.

If the wood has been quartered, then the annual rings are to be seen as straight lines running parallel along the whole length of the board. If the wood is cut in the second way, they appear as wavy lines running diagonally across the board.

The soundboard is invariably cut from quartered wood. The connoisseur should note carefully whether the annual rings run parallel and fade out towards the edges. It is of less importance whether they are close to one another or not. It is more important, however, that they should as far as possible run symmetrically on both sides: closer to each other in the centre and with the distance between the lines gradually increasing towards the edges. This is why the soundboard always consists of two separate pieces.

In the case of the back it is immaterial whether it is made in one or two pieces—at least if it is cut from quartered wood, as is generally the case. If, however, the wood is cut from the trunk in a different way, then preference is given to making the back out of one piece, as otherwise the annual rings running in opposite directions would make a restless, less handsome whole.

Amati preferred to make the back from parallel-cut wood; Stradivarius also did this before 1690, sometimes only the back, on other occasions also the ribs and the scroll. The other parts he cut, as did Amati, from quartered wood. With but few exceptions these backs were by Stradivarius made out of one piece, by Amati, on the other hand, often in two pieces.

As a rule the violin maker uses three different kinds of wood: pine, maple and ebony. Occasionally he will try other varieties; Stradivarius, for instance, especially in his early period, sometimes used poplar for the back and the side-walls or ribs.

The soundboard, sound-post and bass-bar are cut from pinewood, the back, ribs, neck and bridge from maple. The finger-board, string-holder, pegs, nut and button are made of ebony. When it is realised that there are about 50 to 60 different kinds of pine-trees and an equal number of maples, it will be clear how much knowledge and experience is necessary to become expert on the various good and bad qualities of all these woods. Indeed, it is not sufficient for the violin maker to be able to distinguish good from bad timber, he must also be able to take advantage of the structure of the wood, which is never twice the same. Just as no two people have the same finger-prints, so no two trees have, for example, identical annual rings.

Even with boards which have been sawn from the same trunk an absolutely identical structure is inconceivable. In the one board the annual rings, not to go any further, will be closer together than in another. And if we consider that the soundboard, for instance, will have to be thinner or thicker according as the annual rings are closer to one other or the reverse, it will be obvious that it is impos-

15

STRADIVARIUS' HOUSE IN THE PIAZZA
SAN DOMENICO

sible to produce two absolutely identical violins, even if the back and soundboard are cut from the same trunk. Every operation that does not take into account the structure and texture of the wood will produce uncertain results. This partly explains why a reproduction, however accurate the imitation, of an old violin that has been played, will always sound different from the original model. In order to obtain the same result one would have, to begin with, to use for the copy material of exactly the same structure as the original—which is at once quite out of the question. But even if the copy could not be distinguished visually in any respect from the original, its tone would still be different because the old violin had been played upon for a long time, and it is a proven fact that playing on it greatly affects the tone of an instrument. Its age alone plays a very secondary rôle. When at Milan in 1816 Ludwig Spohr played at the house of Count Salabue upon two magnificent Stradivarius violins, he subsequently wrote about them in his autobiography as follows: "The tone is full and strong, but new and woody, and in order to be excellent they must be played upon for at least ten years"—which again proves that it is not age but mainly playing upon it for a long period that can bring out all the possibilities of an instrument.

In 1680 Stradivarius moved with his family to No. 2, Piazza San Domenico. This roomy house, with three storeys, right opposite the entrance to the Church of San Domenico, was built, according to

16

the old Italian custom, round the high *cortile*, the court, which reached as high as the roof and in which there was a well (see sketch plan on p. 17). On the roof there was a sort of room with open walls, through which the wind could play. In this *seccadous*, as it is called in the dialect of Cremona, both linen and fruit were set out to dry. The story goes that in the favourable season Stradivarius would work there and also hung up his newly-varnished instruments to dry. As a rule one could see him sitting in the shop which he had fitted up downstairs in the front room facing the street, a quiet, zealous and industrious worker who, never satisfied with his results, right up to the very end of his life continued to aspire to ever greater heights.

Alas, not a single incontestably authentic portrait of the master has been preserved. We know, among other things, a medallion of him made in 1691 by Francesco Gialdisi which is now in the possession of Pietro Anelli at Cremona. Gialdisi, a painter of flowers and

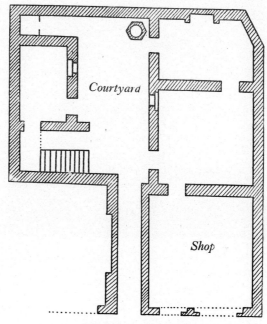

Piazza S. Domenico

GROUND-PLAN OF STRADIVARIUS' HOUSE IN THE PIAZZA SAN DOMENICO

still-lifes born at Parma about the year 1650, died at Cremona after 1720. It is therefore quite possible that he painted Stradivarius from life.

All other portraits or representations of Stradivarius known to us are based on pure fantasy. One of the best-known portraits of this type is certainly the painting by Ed. Hammann, dating from the latter half of the 19th century, preserved in the Museo Civico at Cremona. In this painting we see Stradivarius in his workshop, bent in deep meditation over a violin. Following tradition Hammann has pictured him as a tall thin man with sharp features and long hair. There are

17

ANTONIUS STRADIVARIUS

Copper engraving by A. Morilleron from a painting by Ed. Hammann in the Museo Civico at Cremona

unfinished violins on a table in front of him, while against the wall there is a joiner's bench with tools.

Could it only speak, how much this workshop could tell! And then, what of the whole street! Next door to Stradivarius lived his best pupil, Carlo Bergonzi, and next to him again Joseph Guarnerius del Gesù. A short distance further down, beyond a side turning, lived Francesco Ruggeri, and opposite one of the sides of the Church, Nicolas Amati (see plan on p. 19).

How often must these *maestri* of the art of violin making have chosen the little shop in which to meet and discuss the problems that were occupying them all. Stradivarius must have maintained close touch with them, and especially with Nicolas Amati, whom he continued to assist until the latter's death in 1684. But besides this collaboration he must have worked under his own name, entirely indepen-

dently, and the great reputation he had already gained is proved by
the fact that as early as 1682 he received through Michele Monzi, the
Venetian banker, a commission to make a whole series of instruments
for the King of England.

The death of Nicolas Amati will have contributed in no small

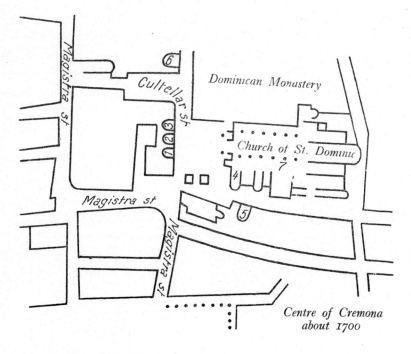

Centre of Cremona
about 1700

1 Antonio Stradivarius
2 Carlo Bergonzi
3 Guarneri del Gesù
4 Chapel of the Rosary, in which Stradivarius was buried.
5 Nicolas Amati
6 Francesco Ruggeri
7 Church of St. Dominic

degree to the establishment of Stradivarius' reputation. He then had
the full opportunity to show not only that he would be able to maintain the traditions of the Amati family, but also that he would be
able, thanks to his rare gifts and fertile initiative, to raise to a higher
level the whole art of violin making.

At first, however, he remained faithful to tradition. Though in the
years 1684–5 a great advance is to be observed, both in the treatment

19

of the form and in the construction of his instruments, the character of his work remained unchanged. He made his violins somewhat larger than before, however, nearer to the 'Great Amati model'. Remarkably enough, this was actually a retrograde step in as far as in some of his instruments he made the ribs heavy and broad, as Nicolas Amati had already done in a number of his violins between 1640 and 1650. Nor did Stradivarius' methods show any great change in the next five years; a few of his instruments differ from one another only in dimensions and minor details. The scroll, to mention one of these, frequently varies; sometimes it is rather too small and sometimes too large in relation to the whole. Sometimes all the dimensions are greater than usual, while other instruments, though they are of full length, are on the other hand narrower and have shallower ribs. In the main, however, the form remained "à l'Amati", as is expressed in the name later given to these instruments.

This name' Amati model' must not be understood wrongly, however, for it is only intended to indicate that these particular instruments betray in a greater or less degree the influence of Amati. In no respect whatsoever are they to be regarded as imitations.

In the year 1690 Stradivarius apparently felt that the time had come for him to free himself entirely from the influence of Amati and to proceed to realise the ideas which for a long time had been slumbering in him. Breaking with tradition, he now introduced reforms more radical than ever before both in the construction, form and dimensions of his instruments.

As had been the case with his predecessors, Stradivarius also had always aimed principally at perfection of tone. He had not laid the emphasis on sonority and carrying power, for in those days the need for this had not yet been felt. On the contrary, practical requirements demanded instruments with a volume well adapted to that of the other instruments then generally used, such as the lute, the clavichord, the harpsichord, the transverse or German flute, the recorder or English flute and the viola da gamba, all of which only produced a modest volume of sound. They were played mainly in small rooms—in the domestic circle, for example, or in the Collegia Musica (or musical societies)—and for this purpose their volume was perfectly adequate. Large concert halls and orchestras consisting of large numbers of performers were then still unknown. Violins too were thus built with a very beautiful but thin tone and for this

THE "TOSCANA" STRADIVARIUS, 1690

purpose a small, fairly high-arched model was eminently suitable.

With his great foresight Stradivarius had realised that in the long run greater demands would be made upon the violin in regard to volume and sonority, and he grasped the fact that such requirements could be met only by means of violins of a larger, only slightly arched model. His acquaintance with the larger and less highly arched models of Maggini, his talented *confrère* at Brescia, probably inspired him to combine in a single instrument the exceptional sonority and fullness of tone of the Maggini violins and the brilliant, soft, noble tone that characterised the Amati instruments. At all events, the influence of Maggini is to be observed in the model which he then designed, the so-called 'patron allongé'. This name is due to the fact that Stradivarius here curved the sides in more than ever before or

21

VIOLA BY STRADIVARIUS, 1696

later, the model thereby becoming somewhat elongated in form.

No instrument of this period demonstrates more clearly how brilliantly Stradivarius succeeded in his efforts than the so-called "Toscana" violin, which dates from 1690. This instrument surpasses all its predecessors not only by reason of its extraordinarily beautiful tone, but especially by the fullness, volume and sonority of its tone. This violin owes its name to the fact that Stradivarius was commissioned to make it by Cosimo de Medici, Grand Duke of Tuscany.

From a purely technical point of view Stradivarius was now at the very height of his powers. The extreme accuracy with which the sound-holes are cut, the marvellously beautiful scroll, the exceedingly delicate work of the inlaid ribs, in short, the entire finish of this instrument, marks its maker as one of the greatest craftsmen the world has ever known. No single violin maker has ever excel-

22

led him in this respect, and only very few have equalled him.

By introducing his new model Stradivarius also proved that he possessed a considerable amount of courage. It was courageous because there was as yet no need for such instruments, and the difference in sound from the instruments of the day was very great. Only gradually, as in the course of the 18th century music moved more and more from the domestic circle to the public concert hall, were the great advantages of these new instruments realised. Stradivarius was in no way disconcerted, however; he stuck to his ideals and continued in the new direction. He could well afford it, anyhow, for he had proved himself not only a great artist but also a good business man. Commissions had reached him from all sorts of countries; he had had to make instruments for various princes and other personages. And he had done well out of it, for in those days his prosperity was so great that even to-day they still say in Cremona 'as rich as Stradivarius'.

It is not only to his violins but also to his violoncellos and violas that Stradivarius owes his fame. The list of instruments decorated with inlaid-work given by Hill also mentions a viola and a violoncello.

Of the violas Hill has only actually seen ten, but he readily admits that it is quite possible that several others may have escaped his attention. The number was in any case not very large, and Hill thinks that the reason for this must be looked for in the fact that in the days of Stradivarius the demand for violas was very small. The trios for two violins and figured bass published by Corelli at the end of the 17th century had become so popular that for a long time this setting dominated chamber music.

Only in the latter half of the 18th century, when the string quartet and string trio (violin, viola and violoncello) came to the fore, did the demand for violas increase. The violas by Gasparo da Salò and the Amatis which were still in circulation in the days of Stradivarius seem to have been sufficient in number to meet the demand.

Gasparo da Salò, Maggini and their contemporaries—in the second half of the 16th and the first half of the 17th centuries, that is—had shown preference for an instrument of very large size. Later, in the second half of the 17th century, it would seem that, thanks to the efforts of the brothers Antonio and Jerome Amati, a smaller model became the fashion, probably for the convenience of the violinists

23

who also played the viola and preferred that the two instruments should not differ too much in size.

Stradivarius' oldest viola known to us dates from 1672 and is therefore of the smaller size, being built entirely according to the traditions of the Amatis. It is not till 1690 that we again encounter two large instruments, the so-called "Toscana" violas, which as regards their form stand somewhat apart. They are even larger than those of Gasparo da Salò but they are not built on the model of the 'patron allongé' which, as we have seen, Stradivarius designed in this year. All his later violas were built entirely according to the principles of this model, so that there is very little difference in timbre between the various violas made by him. That they do, however, differ considerably in timbre and tone from those of Gasparo da Salò and Amati is due to the 'patron allongé' in respect of which Stradivarius differed entirely from all his predecessors. While in the first place their violas excel by their great volume and deep tone, we are struck by the fact that Stradivarius' instruments approach the violin in volume and tone. The disadvantage of this is that, when combined with two violins and a violoncello in a quartet, the G and C strings especially lack the necessary sonority, so that often the player can only with difficulty hold his own against his fellow performers. Moreover, the excessive similarity in the timbre of the violins and the violas means that the desired variety of tone-colour is lacking. To this should be added the circumstance that composers frequently give to the viola solo passages which obviously sound to better advantage on instruments possessing the true viola character. Nevertheless a viola by Stradivarius taken by itself always compels great admiration by its lovely, pure and soul-stirring tone, while the finish is in no respect inferior to that of Stradivarius' other masterpieces.

In comparison with the violas, of which Stradivarius made so few, a comparatively large number of violoncellos made by him is known. In this instrument in particular he reached a level which none of his colleagues was ever able to approach. But this degree of skill and perfection he only acquired after long years of study and meditation; it was not till 1700 that his great genius was able to develop fully in this direction also.

Introduced about the year 1600, the violoncello was at first chiefly used in church music, instead of the viola da gamba, either to play the bass part in polyphonic music or to accompany the recitatives.

24

STRADIVARIUS' HANDWRITING

It was also used in processions. In order to be able to play it while moving, the performer carried it in front of him slung on a cord.

The large space of a church required in the first place that the violoncello should have a powerful sound, which is naturally produced by the largest possible model. This did not make it any easier to play, but in those days the demands on the performer were not very exacting; they played, in fact, chiefly in the first position. At that time it was not yet in use as a solo instrument but when, in the second half of the 17th century, the violoncello came more and more to be used as such the instrument makers made efforts to make it easier to play, which in the first place could be achieved by making a smaller model. Nevertheless the larger model persisted for a considerable time side by side with the smaller and only gradually did it disappear, probably because for quite a long time the Church remained its principal patron. Francesco Ruggeri, for instance, still made a far greater number of large violoncellos than of smaller ones, and it was only about the time of Stradivarius' death that the violin makers definitely gave up the larger model.

Stradivarius himself only devoted his full attention to the construction of the violoncello after 1680, probably as a result of the commissions which he then received from princes for the supply of entire string quartets as well as of violoncellos alone. Hill assumes that between the years 1680 and 1699 Stradivarius must have made at least twenty-five. Remarkably enough, however, they are all without exception of the larger format. Was this because performers still on the whole preferred these or because the instruments were intended exclusively for the churches or the orchestras attached to the princely palaces? Or was Stradivarius when he made his violoncellos still too much under the influence of the Amati tradition? We do not know, but it is a fact in any case that the oldest violoncello known to have been made by him is still entirely under the influence of Amati. It dates from the year 1684 and is a unique example of its kind. It is built on the principles of a violoncello and yet Stradivarius had apparently visualised the instrument as a sort of viola da gamba: the whole construction is massive, particularly the ribs, corners and scroll, while a fifth hole in the pegbox proves clearly that it was originally fitted with five strings like the viola da gamba.

Like his predecessors, Stradivarius was always careful to make the outward shape of his violoncellos match that of his violins. In no

26

single respect, whether in the position or shape of the sound-holes, the outline of the instrument or the design of the scroll, can the slightest deviation be observed. For example, the violoncello that matches the Toscana violin was also made entirely on the 'patron allongé'. Peculiarly enough, however, this instrument lacks the sonorous tone and full volume of the Toscana violin. The so-called "Aylesford" violoncello of 1696 is also characteristic of its period.

The supreme craftsmanship revealed especially in these last two instruments must have filled Stradivarius' colleagues with great respect and compelled them to admit that a giant had arisen among them to whom they would sooner or later have to bend the knee.

And yet it is very doubtful whether modern violoncellists are of the same opinion. They mostly ask rather for a powerful than a beautiful tone, although they are of course not indifferent to softness and beauty of tone. Their ideal of tone has changed with circumstances, and they find it difficult to be satisfied any longer with an instrument of weak tone. Such instruments—and among these are the Stradivarius violoncellos dating from before 1700—they value more as curiosities than as instruments to be played on to-day. Modern violoncello makers concentrate in the first place on giving the A string—the principal melody string—a powerful, penetrating tone and on giving the C string as metallic a tone as possible, the two middle strings naturally having to be sacrificed more or less to these requirements.

Till 1699 Stradivarius continued to make violoncellos on the old model, and after that he went over to a smaller size, as we shall see later.

With his violins also Stradivarius did not make such rapid progress as he could have wished. An even higher ideal floated before his mind's eye, and he was determined not to rest until he had achieved it. He therefore started to make a fresh series of experiments. In the years 1691–2, for instance, he made his violins larger than ever, but the following year he returned to the 'patron allongé' of 1690, retaining, however, the exceptional length of the instruments of the preceding two years. Apart from a few exceptions he adhered to this till 1698. Then, remarkably enough, he suddenly reverted to the 'Amati' model of before 1690, though with a few slight modifications. In 1699 he again worked on the 'patron allongé' and then, as far as can be ascertained, he said good-bye to it for good. The 'Amati' model then again became his favourite, remaining so until 1703.

After having been married 31 years Stradivarius lost his wife in the year 1698. She was buried on 25 May in that year. However, he did not long remain a widower, for on 24 August of the following year he married Antonia Maria Zambelli, who was some twenty years his junior.

Of his first marriage there were still five children alive, namely, Giulio, Francesco, Catterina, Allessandro and Omobono, who were at the time 31, 28, 25, 22 and 19 years of age respectively. Giulio, Catterina and perhaps also Allessandro were probably, in view of their age, no longer living in the parental house. On the other hand, Francesco and Omobono were probably still living at home, for they not only assisted Stradivarius in his work but eventually succeeded him.

Of the marriage with Antonia five children were born, four boys and a girl. The girl, Francesca, born on 19 September 1700, died at the age of twenty. G. B. Giuseppe, born on 6 November 1701, died on 8 July in the following year. Nor did G. B. Martino, born 11 November 1703, attain a ripe age, for he died on 1 November 1727. On the other hand, his brother Giuseppe, born 27 October 1704, who became a priest, and Paolo, born on 26 January 1708, a cloth merchant, reached the ages of 77 and 68 respectively.

In the year 1704 Stradivarius seems at last to have reached his goal. Everything he made then is of the highest quality. The ideal Stradivarius model was designed, and he was to stick to it until 1720. Only in minor details can any deviations be observed. He did, it is true, occasionally make an instrument of smaller size, but apparently only at the special request of a client. The tone, too, seems now to have fully satisfied Stradivarius, for all his violins of this period are distinguished by the same extraordinarily brilliant, full and powerful tone. In this 'golden age', as the years up to 1720 are usually called, Stradivarius made a number of masterpieces which in their highly original conception were never to be excelled, either by himself or by any other violin maker.

Stradivarius must have felt very sure of his ground to follow his own ideas so deliberately at a time when the tone qualities of the Amati and the Stainer instruments were still so much preferred. He

THE "BETTS" STRADIVARIUS, 1704

must have been thoroughly convinced that the time was near in which his own productions would be preferred above all others.

One of Stradivarius' most glorious masterpieces is the so-called "Betts" violin of 1704. The wood for this instrument he must have chosen with exceptional care and sensitiveness: for the soundboard he used an extremely light pine with an even number of annual rings and for the back a magnificent maple. The arch of the rather flat soundboard has been harmoniously adapted to the texture of the wood. The sound-holes are exquisitely cut, of noble line and unsurpassable elegance. The scroll is equally fine and not so deeply carved as hitherto. The corners are prominent and broad, the whole instrument having a most elegant appearance. Over a golden-yellow ground varnish a bright red varnish has been added, producing a brilliant brownish tint. The whole is a masterpiece of perfect beauty.

The "Betts" Stradivarius owes its name to a remarkable incident. On a certain day in the year 1825 a very poorly dressed man offered a violin for sale to the violin maker Betts of London. Betts, out of pity for the man's circumstances, bought the neglected instrument, without examining it carefully, for a guinea. How great was his surprise and joy, however, when he discovered that it was one of the finest masterpieces of Stradivarius, made in 1704. In spite of diligent inquiries he never succeeded in tracing the man who had sold it to him, to let him participate in his good fortune. The man's name was never discovered, so that nothing is known of the adventures of the violin before 1825. Later, after many wanderings about Europe, it came eventually, in the first quarter of the 20th century, into the possession of a wealthy collector in Amsterdam.

After 1704 one masterpiece succeeded another in almost unbroken succession. It is worth relating a few interesting particulars about some of these world-famous instruments.

In the first place there is the so-called "Viotti" Stradivarius, of 1709, on which, as its name suggests, the celebrated Italian violinist J. B. Viotti played until his death. Later Arnold Rosé bought this instrument for 27,000 guilders (at that time about £2250).

Then we must mention two violins of 1715, the "Alard" Stradivarius, so called because for a long time it was the property of the French violinist Delphin Alard, and the "Emperor". The latter was for many years the property of the English collector Gillott, who would never allow the precious instrument to be touched by any other hands than his own. This undoubtedly meant that for a long time the violin was withheld from its natural use and one frequently hears such action condemned, but we must not forget that it is to such maniacs as Gillott that we owe it that at least a few masterpieces have been preserved for us in perfect condition. Ultimately the "Emperor" came once more into worthy hands, for the famous Bohemian virtuoso Jan Kubelik, who paid 50,000 guilders or about £4200 for it, enraptured his audiences with it.

The most famous of Stradivarius' violins is the so-called "Messiah", which dates from 1716. It owes its unusual name to the following story. In the first half of the 19th century there lived at Fontenetto, in the neighbourhood of Milan, a young joiner, Tarisio by name,

30

THE "ALARD" STRADIVARIUS, 1715

whose hobby it was to collect violins. He journeyed from village to village and from city to city, always on the track of instruments by Italian masters, whose names were at that time practically unknown but which, thanks mainly to Tarisio, were later to become world-famous. Guided by his connoisseur's eye he was soon able to gather together a most valuable collection of old Italian masterpieces, including a violin which he had purchased from the estate of Count Cozio di Salabue, who had originally purchased it in 1775 from Stradivarius' son Paolo.

Although as a passionate collector Tarisio could only part from his treasures with difficulty, he one day resolved to go to Paris and try to dispose of a few of his less valuable pieces. In 1827 after a long journey on foot, with his instruments in a sack on his back, he arrived in Paris. There he called on the violin maker Aldric and although Tarisio, well knowing what his instruments were worth,

THE "DUPORT" STRADIVARIUS, 1711 (VIOLONCELLO)

demanded fairly high prices, Aldric could not resist the temptation to purchase the entire collection. He also begged Tarisio to return as soon as possible with a fresh consignment. A second visit to Paris led Tarisio, however, to Chanot and Vuillaume, who were as delighted as Aldric had been. Again Tarisio did good business, returning to Italy without a single instrument. Astute business man that he was, on this occasion also he had not taken with him his finest instruments. He had repeatedly promised, however, that when he came to Paris again he would bring with him the violin which had belonged to Count Cozio di Salabue, a Stradivarius that surpassed anything of his known in France up to that time, but again and again he disap-

32

pointed Vuillaume. On one occasion, when Tarisio was in his shop again bragging about his divine Stradivarius, Alard, who happened to be present, exclaimed: "Vraiment, Monsieur Tarisio, votre violon est comme le Messie des Juifs; on l'attend toujours, mais il ne paraît jamais". It is to these words that the violin owes its peculiar name, though it is also known as the Salabue Stradivarius.

Tariso could not, however, part with this instrument. He never took it with him to Paris and until his death he surrounded it with loving care as his most precious possession. When Tarisio died, in 1854, Vuillaume at once hastened to Milan and was able to secure the violin from the heirs for about 40,000 guilders (about £ 3,330). Now, however, Vuillaume fell a victim to the same passion as Tarisio: he could not bear to part with the violin and he kept it, indeed, until his death in 1875. It then changed hands a few times, eventually becoming the property of Messrs. Hill of London, who a few years ago presented it to the City of London.

It was in 1699 that Stradivarius at last began to make smaller violoncellos. We only know one specimen of that year and this has unfortunately suffered so much in the course of time that its original qualities can no longer be clearly distinguished. However, a violoncello of 1700, which is known as the "Cristiani", thanks to its excellent condition is perfectly able to give us a clear picture of the details of Stradivarius' small model. As with his violins of this period, the curve of this violoncello is also flatter than before. The splendid plum-red varnish enhances in no slight degree the beauty of this masterpiece.

In the following year, 1701, Stradivarius again produced one of his greatest masterpieces, the so-called "Servais" violoncello. Then follow six years during which, as far as we can ascertain, no violoncellos left Stradivarius' hands. Had he received no commissions or was he, not yet entirely satisfied with the splendid results he had already obtained, still meditating improvements? However it may be, in 1707 he produced a violoncello which put all his earlier models in the shade, presenting us with the ideal violoncello of the future. This model, again slightly smaller, excels in beauty of form, purity of style and refinement of finish. The tone of an instrument such as this, brilliant, full and tender, and yet powerful in volume, will be sought for in vain among the instruments of any other master.

Antonius Stradiuarius Cremonenfis Alumnus
Nicolaij Amati, Faciebat Anno 1666

Antonius Stradiuarius Cremonenfis
Faciebat Anno 1667

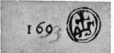
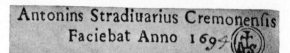

1672   1689   1668

1669   1693   Antonins Stradiuarius Cremonenfis
Faciebat Anno 1694

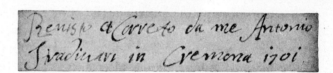

1698   Antonius Stradiuarius Cremonenfis
Faciebat Anno 1699   1698

1700   Renisp a Carveto da me Antonio
Stradiuari in Cremona 1701

1701   1703   1704

1708   1709   1711

1713   1714

STRADIVARIUS' LABELS

34

1715

1716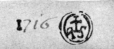

Antonius Stradiuarius Cremonenſis
Faciebat Anno 1717

1718

Reuiſto, e Corretto da me Antonio
Stradiuari in Cremona 1719
e fatto il Coperchio

1720

1722

1723

1727

Antonius Stradivarius Cremonenſis
Faciebat Anno 1732
de Anni 9

Antonius Stradivarius Cremonenſis
Faciebat Anno 1736
D ANNi 92
92

Antonius Stradivarius Cremonenſis
Faciebat Anno 1736
D'Ann..
D'ANNi 92

Antonius Stradivarius Cremonenſis
Faciebat Anno 1737
D'Anni 93

Sotto la Diſciplina d'Antonio
Stradiuari F. in Cremona 1737

Omobonus Stradiuarius Filus Antonÿ
Cremone fecit Anno 1740: oT's

Franciſcus Stradivarius Cremonenſis
Filius Antonii faciebat Anno 1742

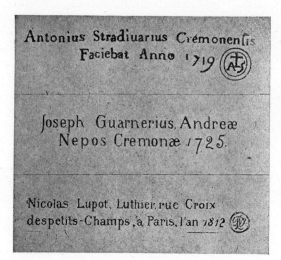

FORGED LABELS

Until the end of his long life Stradivarius was to remain faithful to this model. There are, it is true, a couple of violoncellos of the years subsequent to 1730 which are of a somewhat smaller and different shape, but these are largely if not entirely the work of his assistants.

Wherein lies the secret of these results, unsurpassed to this day? Some people wish us to believe that Stradivarius possessed an extraordinary acoustic sense which guided him in the choice of the wood he used, and that his instruments owe their unparalleled qualities of tone chiefly to the special qualities of these woods.

But how then is it to be explained that the instruments which Stradivarius made before 1684 were nevertheless veritable masterpieces although, generally speaking, the wood leaves so much to be desired that a modern violin maker would certainly have rejected it, though he might still have been able to make a good instrument from it?

Was Stradivarius himself so thoroughly convinced that the quality of the wood was of secondary importance that in the earlier part of his career he paid so little attention to it? I do not think so, for in his later years it was just to the selection of the wood that he devoted the greatest care. It is possible that at first he could not obtain any better wood, or that it was too expensive for him in view of the modest prices which at the time he could demand for his instruments. Whichever of these possibilities is the true one, his violins prove repeatedly that the quality of the wood was not the chief condition for the success of his work. And, moreover, if this had really been the case, what is there to prevent the modern violin maker from using equally excellent wood? The claim that the varieties of wood available at the time of Stradivarius are no longer obtainable has long proved to be untenable. Indeed, the modern violin maker has in this respect

36

WELL FROM STRADIVARIUS' HOUSE AND STRADIVARIUS' TOMBSTONE,
both in the Museo Civico at Cremona

the advantage of the old Italians, for they had to seek out the timber for themselves in the forests and to dry it for long periods before it could be used. The modern violin maker, on the other hand, need only call on his timber merchant in order to be able to choose woods, well-dried and cut into boards ready for use, from all kinds of excellent varieties imported from every part of the world. If when sorting out a consignment his knowledge of timber should leave him in the lurch, then the prices marked on the various specimens will certainly help to put him on the right track.

It has also been thought that the varnish which Stradivarius used must have been the cause of the unsurpassed results he obtained. What volumes have been written about that varnish! It is said that he always anxiously guarded his varnish recipes and that he took the secret of his varnish with him to the grave. It was thus only a question of discovering this secret in order at a single stroke to solve the riddle of his superiority. That this mysterious secret has already been repeatedly revealed goes without saying, but these various discoveries have descended to their grave-oblivion. No, that varnish secret is a legend. In the days of Stradivarius, and also before and after his time, the various recipes for varnish were certainly not kept a secret. How can there have been any question of a secret, seeing that practically all Italian violin makers, right down to the second half of the 18th century, had excellent varnish at their disposal? Indeed, it was not only the Italians who knew how to make excellent varnish mixtures, but also Germans, and even the Dutchman Hendrik Jacobszoon, who had never been in Italy, was a great master of this art. No, the varnish that Stradivarius used was in no respect of better quality than that of many another violin maker. Good results cannot be obtained, however, with the very best of varnishes unless it is applied to the instruments with expert knowledge and skill, at a certain temperature and in a certain number of layers. Now Stradivarius must without doubt have been a past master in this art and to this he owes his magnificent results, the only secret of which was — his genius.

Naturally the quality of the varnish plays a very important part. If a violin has a good sound before it is varnished, it will undoubtedly be ruined for good by a bad varnish which has, for instance, been laid on too thick, that penetrates too deep into the pores and that eventually hardens into a thick crust. A badly constructed violin,

38

CHURCH OF ST. DOMINIC AT CREMONA

on the other hand, will never turn into a masterpiece even if the finest varnish is applied with the utmost care. The varnish enhances the beauty of an instrument not a little, but its real task is to protect the violin against wear, the influence of moisture, and so on. The great secret of preparing varnish is to make a mixture which will not have a detrimental effect on the vibrating of the wood. Varnish must be neither too hard nor too plastic and it must be transparent, elastic and brilliant.

That a visible deterioration in the quality of the varnish of Italian violins is to be observed in the second half of the 18th century must not be attributed to the loss of secret recipes but chiefly to the fact that the great demand for violins in those days induced the violin makers to use spirit varnish instead of oil varnish. Spirit varnish dries far more rapidly than oil varnish, thus enabling the instruments to be supplied more quickly. The result was that the violin makers gradually lost the art of making oil varnish and applying it to their instruments. When, later on, the demand for such varnishes returned they naturally lacked the skill and practice to make and apply it. In modern times, however, most violin makers have entirely regained the mastery of this important branch of their art.

39

From the foregoing it has, I think, been sufficiently demonstrated that Stradivarius had no better wood and varnish at his disposal than his colleagues. And if, moreover, we know that in the treatment of the soundboard and back, the dimensions and placing of the bass-bar, the inlaid work of the ribs, in fact in the whole construction of his instruments, he followed the main lines laid down by his predecessors, then it will be clear that he did not possess any particular constructional secrets. The extraordinary results which he obtained he owed entirely to his great genius, which was able to combine together in complete harmony both wood and varnish, dimensions and general shape and all the other incalculable factors.

In 1720 Stradivarius attained his seventy-sixth year. One would have expected him to rest gradually on his laurels, or at least that he would have left the greater part of the work to his two sons and to his talented pupil, Carlo Bergonzi. He could still have advised his pupils and supervised their work. Nothing of the kind; it seems as if old age could get no hold on him. Perfectly sound in mind and body, he retained at that great age a firm hand which enabled him to maintain his work at the high level to which he had brought it. He allowed no one to help him in his work: in no instrument built between 1720 and 1725 can any trace of the work of others be observed. It is, naturally, possible that his pupils had done the rough work for him, but if so he always removed all traces of their work in the finishing of the instrument. His sons and Bergonzi may possibly also have relieved him by making unimportant accessories such as fingerboards, bridges and string-holders, and by executing repairs, but this would only be to permit him to devote himself entirely to the actual building of his instruments.

Stradivarius would not have been himself if, even at that advanced age, he had not quietly continued his experiments. In the years 1720 to 1722 he again designed a new model, which gave his instruments a totally different tone. Although these are of normal size, they make, owing to the more or less angular form of the upper and lower edges, and the flat arch of the soundboard and back, an unusually robust and sturdy, and somewhat inelegant, impression. The "Blunt" of 1721 and the "Brandt" and the "Chaponay" of 1722, typical examples of this new style, possess a particularly powerful and penetrating tone with a more or less metallic timbre that reminds one of the instruments of Joseph Guarnerius del Gesù and of Carlo Bergonzi, which were undoubtedly inspired by this model of Stradivarius.

These characteristics dominate in most of the instruments produced in the last years of Stradivarius' life. In the finish of the ribs, the corners, the sound-holes, scroll and inlaidwork we miss that extreme degree of accuracy to which he had so accustomed us. The pinewood, alas, has no longer been selected with such great care as had been the case ten years earlier, and even the varnish is on the whole of poorer quality, but the workmanship of these instruments is nevertheless still of a high order.

The violins of this period have been the favourite instruments of such virtuosos as Baillot, Kreutzer, Wilhelmj and Ysaye, because in the second half of the 19th century these artists wished to impress their audiences by a powerful, sonorous tone. An exception to this

SCREW-HOLDER OF A STRADIVARIUS GUITAR

rule was Pablo de Sarasate, who attached greater value to other qualities. He also played on a Stradivarius of this period, of 1724, but one which differed from the other instruments of those years, for it excelled rather by its brilliance, clarity and distinction than by its power and resonance.

In the years 1725 to 1730 we see Stradivarius still working on quietly. Many of his productions of those days bear, it is true, signs of decline, but at the same time there are some which fill us with admiration at the intellectual and physical vitality of the aged artist. The arching of the plates is occasionally flatter than ever before, and then again it is sometimes exactly as in the years 1720–25. Alas, the quality of the wood and also of the varnish leaves increasingly more to be desired. And yet how admirable these instruments are in comparison with those of many other well-known makers!

Much of his beloved work he had now gradually to leave to others, but the most important tasks he still performed himself, and the tone of the instruments of this period is on the whole not inferior to that of many a specimen dating from an earlier period. Apparently highly satisfied with these results, Stradivarius has with pride mentioned his age on some of his labels: "Fatto de Anni 83", etc.

Violin makers had of old made a custom of mentioning on a label affixed to the inside of the back their name, the town where they lived, and the year in which the instrument was made, sometimes also their birthplace and the name of their master. If they had not done this, it is most probable that not many names of violin makers would have come down to us, or, even if we had known the names, we should not have been able to determine who had been the maker of any particular instrument. Genuine labels are therefore invaluable for the identification both of the maker and of particular instruments. I must unfortunately speak of 'genuine' labels, because there are so many false ones in circulation. Many a violin maker has, for instance, reproduced exactly the work of some great master or other and stuck in it an equally imitated label,

ROSETTE OF A STRADIVARIUS GUITAR

thus making possible an ingenious swindle. Nevertheless, not every one of such acts must be deemed an attempt to deceive. In the 15th century it was the custom not only in Italy but also, for example, in England, for apprentices who copied the work of their masters also to stick in the instrument a copy of their master's label, without any other intention than to state that their work, including the label, should be looked upon as a faithul copy. That they had no intention to deceive is proved by the fact that they frequently added their own label elsewhere on the instrument. Even Vuillaume, the greatest copyist of the 19th century, on occasion added to his instruments a label by Stradivarius or Guarnerius but no one who knew him would dare to assert that he did so with intent to deceive. He always dated

42

VIOLIN BY OMOBONO STRADIVARIUS, 1740

the Stradivarius labels 1717 and did not even take the trouble, any more than the Italians had done, to copy the text correctly. Moreover, he made a habit of numbering his instruments in the centre of the back, a thing that neither Stradivarius nor Guarnerius ever did. Vuillaume would never have done this if he had wished to create the impression that his violins were authentic works by Stradivarius and other masters.]

[The position is totally different, however, with the labels affixed to instruments by dealers in old masterpieces. With them, deception must have been the only motive. It even seems that Tarisio started the game. Several at least of the instruments offered by him for sale in Paris bore labels which could not possibly have been placed there by the makers themselves. The intention was obvious. The great demand for old Italian masterpieces, particularly for those of Amati

43

and Stradivarius, induced him to mark the work of less famous Italians with the labels of these two masters, with a view to disposing of these instruments as genuine works. He but too frequently succeeded in doing so, because the purchasers, who were mostly inexperienced, could not appreciate the slight differences between the work of a master and that of his assistants and pupils. And if he was thus most successful in this fraud, so also were others, so that it was not long before there was in circulation a large number of violins bearing false labels. In the long run this deception was bound to come to light, for men like Vuillaume and Hill, who had made a special study of the old Italian violin makers, raised their voices in warning, calling attention to this steadily increasing abuse. The result was that the label, without which nothing had been genuine, was suddenly denounced, and no one any longer attached any value to it. This went too far, however, for it is a fact that nearly all the instruments by the really great masters have retained their original label, for what would have been the advantage of affixing a different label on the work of a Stradivarius or a Guarnerius? The value would only have been diminished. But with instruments of the second or third rank caution is most advisable with regard to the authenticity of their labels. I am not thinking of the coarse imitations of famous Italian masters usually found in cheap factory violins, for there the imitation is too blatant to be misleading. In such cases the manufacturer only wished to indicate in what style the violins were made. These labels, printed in strips (see p. 36), are on the market.

We have already observed that practically all Stradivarius' instruments still bear their original label. And yet people have managed to tamper with them. Stradivarius himself, unfortunately, almost invited it. On his first labels he had printed, unthinkingly, the first three figures of the year—166—so that in the seventies he had either to use new labels or erase the last 6 as well as he could and write a 7 in ink in its place. Thrifty as he was, Stradivarius chose the latter method. After 1680 it was even easier, for he only had to change the 6 in ink into an 8. From 1690 on, it is true, he had fresh labels printed but still with the last 6, which he faithfully altered into a 9. There was otherwise every reason for him to reject this label, for a mistake had been made in the name Antonius, which had been printed as 'Antonins', probably by setting the 'u' upside down. But all this made no difference to Stradivarius and it was not till nearly

44

VIOLIN BY CARLO BERGONZI, 1733

the end of the century, when he again needed fresh labels, that he corrected this mistake and also only printed the first figure of the year, namely 1. After this date he always added the other three figures in ink. The monogram, which does not appear on some of his labels, Stradivarius must always have added by means of a separate stamp. For the rest, at each reprint the labels became steadily coarser. The label dated 1719 is interesting, for it seems as if Stradivarius also undertook repairs; on this label the first two figures are printed. In 1729, in a fresh printing of his labels, he had the consonantal 'u' in his name changed into a 'v'.

Stradivarius' carelessness in regard to his labels has in no small measure encouraged forgery. The entirely mistaken view that the products of Stradivarius' first and last periods are inferior to those of his middle period, for instance, has induced many a dealer to alter the dates on the labels of instruments of the early and later periods into those of what were regarded as Stradivarius' best years. Sometimes only quite a small alteration was required while in other cases the whole series of figures had to be changed; fortunately most of these forgeries were rather clumsily executed, so that the real connoisseur has not been deceived (see pp. 34–35).

In the last years of his life Stradivarius also mentioned his age on his labels, for the first time, as far as we know, on a violin of the year 1732, on which is written "d'anni 89", and for the last time on a violin of 1737, where we find "d'anni 93". These violins Stradivarius apparently made entirely or almost entirely by himself, but most of the instruments of those days are largely the work of his assistants. In these cases he had printed on the label "sotto la disciplina d'Antonio Stradivari" (i.e., under the direction of Antonio Stradivari). He could scarcely suspect that later on dishonest dealers would not hesitate to exchange these labels for old ones of Stradivarius alone in order to pass these instruments off as genuine 'Strads'. Their father's labels were even affixed to instruments which were entirely the work of Omobono or of Francesco. After the death of Stradivarius a number of instruments appeared that had apparently been put together from parts which were mainly the work of Stradivarius himself but assembled and finished by his sons. These instruments naturally also bore forged labels, but fortunately the work of Stradivarius during the last years of his life still bears such a personal character that true connoisseurs have no

THE STRADIVARIUS ROOM IN THE MUSEO CIVICO AT CREMONA

difficulty at all in distinguishing his work from that of his assistants.

In 1730 Stradivarius reached the age of 86 and although he was still able to work he had the year before already taken steps to prepare his last resting place. In doing so Stradivarius again showed that he was not only a careful but a thrifty man, for he did not buy a new grave but took over from the heirs of Francesco Villani, a descendant of a noble Cremonese family, a grave in one of the small chapels of the Church of San Domenico. He did not even turn up his nose at the old gravestone that went with it, for he had the previous names erased and his own carved instead. Unfortunately, traces of the earlier inscriptions are still visible, which gives the whole thing a most improbable appearance. The date 1729 especially, which has remained on the stone, might lead to mistaken conclusions. Later this stone, together with the well from the court of Stradivarius' house, was removed to the Museo Civico at Cremona (see p. 37).

Although Stradivarius had now with every year to leave the making of violins more and more to his assistants, he still occasionally made a violin himself without any help. These are all different in type and character and all without exception give evidence of great

47

decline. In the "Hebeneck" Stradivarius of 1736, for example, the right sound-hole is much higher than the left one, and in the "Müntz" violin the inlaid work has been executed with such a trembling hand and in the cutting the knife has so slipped about in all directions that the groove is about as wide as that of the purfling of a violoncello. The quality of the varnish also deteriorated in these last years. It is laid on too thickly and is particularly lacking in transparency and richness of colour. And yet all these violins, individually considered, are still masterpieces; it was only the lack of a firm hand which prevented Stradivarius from equalling his earlier triumphs. There is nothing wrong with the shape and construction, so that in beauty of tone these instruments are not inferior to the earlier ones. The decline in outward appearance is on the whole so slight that it really only becomes noticeable if instruments of the periods 1710–15 and 1720–25 are placed beside those of 1730–35.

Gradually Stradivarius' strength declined; he could no longer do much work, and the death of his wife on 4 March 1737 was the final blow; he died on 18 December of that year at the age of about 94. He was buried the next day in the Church of San Domenico.

Down to 1869 his relatives and descendants also found their last resting place in this church. By then, however, the church had so fallen into decay, and had become, indeed, a public danger, that it was pulled down and a park laid out where it had stood. This naturally brought to light the grave of Stradivarius, and his mortal remains were then, together with those of others, re-interred somewhere outside the city. In this way the grave of one of Cremona's greatest sons disappeared without anyone bothering any further about it. At the spot where his grave used to be the authorities have set up a memorial stone on which may still be read, by way of explanation, the word 'Privisorio'!

With Stradivarius there passed away the greatest violin maker of all time. His greatness lies not only in the perfection of his creations but above all in the fact that he produced in them the ideal instrument of the future.

The instruments of his predecessors had satisfied entirely all the demands which were made on the violin in their day. Nicolas Amati, basing himself on the traditions of the Cremonese school, had raised the art of violin making to a height beyond which it seemed impossible to bring it. Stradivarius, at first continuing in the direction initiated by Amati, gradually came to the conclusion, thanks to his wonderful foresight, that in the long run still greater demands would be made on the violin, especially as regards sonority and volume. This is why he freed himself at a given moment from the influence of Amati in order to strike out on entirely new paths. With his large, low-arched model designed after 1700 he broke away entirely from the traditions of the old school and created an instrument which with its great volume and sonorous tone was to be the violin of the future. Stradivarius is to be looked upon as marking the culmination of the old school and as the founder of a new order of which he was at the same time the principal representative.

Without Stradivarius the violin would have become the victim of tradition, because it would in the long run have ceased to be able to adapt itself to the requirements of the times. It is thanks to Stradivarius that it has been able to maintain itself till to-day as the Queen of musical instruments.

If at first it was only his pupils who followed him in this new direction, eventually everywhere in Italy and abroad violin makers came to realise that Stradivarius' instruments were the instruments of the future, and it was not long before his post-1700 model became the exemplar of practically every violin maker. Just as in the 17th century the models of Nicolas Amati and Stainer had been imitated by practically every other violin maker, so the Stradivarius violin became the ideal of most violin makers of the 19th century. To approach Stradivarius as near as possible was their

THICKNESS-GAUGE FOR SOUNDBOARD AND BACK

highest endeavour, and although there are among modern violin makers many who work on a so-called model of their own, these nevertheless betray more or less the influence of Stradivarius, and however strongly the personality of the modern maker may be expressed in his work, with regard to the tone his aim is exactly the same as Stradivarius'. Stradivarius' ideal of tone is also that of the modern violin maker. Stradivarius' spirit continues to live among them and will continue to do so until altered times shall once more make different demands on the violin. A new Stradivarius will then have to arise and lead the art of violin making along fresh paths. Until that time comes, however, Stradivarius' creations will remain the *non plus ultra* of the art of violin making.

The most fantastic tales have been circulated with regard to the number of instruments which during three quarters of a century of activity came from Stradivarius' hands. Some people have asserted that there must have been at least three thousand, while others, on the other hand, have been of opinion that the number of genuine Stradivariuses must have been comparatively small, and that most of the instruments which bear his label are imitations.

Hill has studied the whole question thoroughly and after very careful calculations has come to the conclusion that Stradivarius must have built about 1116 instruments, including a few viola da gambas, two dancing master's violins and two guitars, the remainder consisting of violins, violas and violoncellos. That Stradivarius also made a few double basses, as some people believe, Hill denies categorically. The number of violas he estimates at 12 and of violoncellos at 80, so that according to his reckoning Stradivarius must have made about 1016 violins. Of these Hill has traced 540, but he believes that he has only been able to trace 75%, which would mean that there are about 720 in circulation and that in the course of time 300 have been lost in some way or other. Of the 'cellos Hill has actually seen 50 and he presumes that 7 or 8 have escaped his attention, so that about 22 would seem to have been lost. He has probably seen all the violas, and not more than one or two specimens can have escaped him.

On the death of Stradivarius there were in his workshop still 91 violins, 2 violoncellos and a couple of violas, which with the rest of his estate came into the possession of his sons and successors, Francesco and Omobono. In the meantime Bergonzi had established his own workshop in the house next door. Unfortunately, Francesco and Omobono were unable to maintain their father's great reputation; they proved to be his inferiors in every respect. In his book *The*

Violin George Hart says that he is quite unable to understand how instruments by Francesco can ever have been passed off as being by Antonius, for Francesco's instruments are not only much less carefully finished but the entire model, and also the sound-holes, are totally different. He admits, however, that the tone is very fine. Hill declares that he has never seen a violin by Francesco, while on the other hand Lütgendorff, in his book *Die Geigen- und Lautenmacher*, mentions a magnificent violin of 1735 which in 1922 belonged to Karl Prill at Vienna.

Only a single violin by Omobono, dated 1740, is known to us. In 1937 it was to be seen at the exhibition at Cremona (see p. 43). This very characteristic instrument aroused general interest, in spite of its somewhat rough, careless finish.

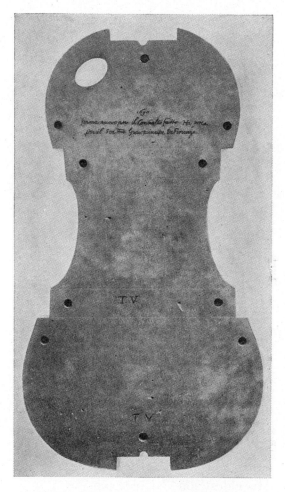

VIOLONCELLO PATTERN BY STRADIVARIUS

After the death of Omobono on 8 June 1742 and of Francesco on 11 May 1743 Stradivarius' house and workshop passed into the possession of Carlo Bergonzi, in whom Stradivarius found a worthy successor. Bergonzi was born at Cremona in 1686 and trained wholly in the school of Stradivarius, though he was not the kind of man to imitate his master blindly. He retained, it is true, the principle of the flat arch but in other respects went his own way. For instance, he made the upper portion of his instruments somewhat longer and the lower portion somewhat broader than Stradivarius had done,

51

thus producing a model that lies somewhere between those of Stradivarius and Joseph Guarnerius del Gesù. The sound-holes, which betray the influence of Guarnerius, Bergonzi placed somewhat higher and closer to the edges. The varnish, sometimes laid on too thickly, is reddish-brown or amber in colour. Thanks to their full noble tone, his instruments are reckoned among the best products of the Cremonese School.

This cannot, alas, be said of the instruments of his son Michel Angelo, who succeeded him after his death in 1747. His instruments follow the lines not only of Stradivarius' large model but also of the models of other masters. Although he used very fine wood and finished his instruments beautifully, he did not attain his father's level. He made comparatively few bowed string instruments, devoting himself early to mandolines and other plucked instruments. His eldest son Nicolo succeeded him in 1765, a comparatively large number of instruments by whom have been preserved; he continued to work entirely along the lines of his father. In finish and tone his instruments approach closely those of Michel Angelo.

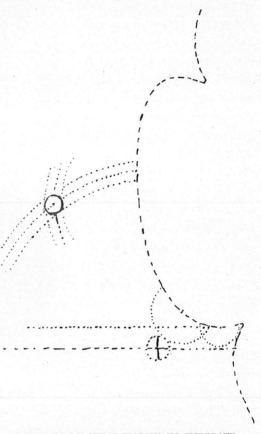

DRAWINGS BY STRADIVARIUS TO INDICATE
POSITION OF SOUND-HOLES

The last descendant of this famous family of violin makers of Cremona, Benedetto Bergonzi, died at Cremona in 1840. He was only of importance, however, as a repairer. He lived until his death in the house of his ancestors, that of Stradivarius also, that is, in the Piazza San Domenico. It is said that Fétis obtained the information concerning Stradivarius and his contemporaries which he used in his biography of Stradivarius from Vuillaume, who in turn had got it via Tarisio from Benedetto Bergonzi.

In this work Fétis states that, according to Vuillaume, Joseph Guarnerius del Gesù, Lorenzo Guadagnini, Francesco Gobetti, Allessandro Gagliano and Michel Angelo Bergonzi were also pupils of Stradivarius, while Hart in his work already cited mentions that this was the case with Guadagnini, Gagliano, Bergonzi and Montagnana.

misura per la forma B per far li occhi del violoncello

Hart asserts, and Hill agrees with him, that Joseph Guarnerius del Gesù was not a pupil of Stradivarius but of his uncle Joseph, the son of Andreas Guarnerius. Moreover Hill believes that if Gobetti and Allessandro Gagliano were really pupils of Stradivarius — which he is very much inclined to doubt—this must have been during Stradivarius' earlier years, for by 1700 both of them were already working on their own, one in Venice, the other in Naples.

As regards Montagnana, Hill is equally sceptical. The fact that Montagnana called his house in Venice "Cremona" naturally proves nothing, and in no respect whatever does his work remind one of the Cremonese School.

With respect to Lorenzo Guadagnini, Hill is less positive in his statements. He recognises the possibility of Lorenzo having been a pupil of Stradivarius and willingly admits that Stradivarius' influence is observable in Lorenzo's work, but he attaches little value to the label that Lorenzo used and that is supposed to be evidence of his really having been a pupil of Stradivarius. The label runs: "Laurentius Guadagnini, fecit Piacentiae, alumnus Antonius Stradivarius 1740". Hill possessed such a label, which had belonged to the well-known collection of Charles Reade (second half of the 19th century). It was gummed on a piece of paper on which Reade had written: "N.B. At Piacenza it was easy to call himself a pupil of Stradivari—he dare not have said so at Cremona". Hill is inclined to agree fully with this verdict of Reade's.

As we have seen, Michel Angelo Bergonzi was a pupil of his father, so that ultimately not a single one of the violin makers mentioned by Fétis and Hart can be accepted without reservation as having been a pupil of Stradivarius. This can only be said with certainty of Stradivarius' own two sons and Carlo Bergonzi.

The house in the Piazza San Domenico in which Stradivarius and Bergonzi made their masterpieces and which for 160 years had been a centre of the art of violin making, remained intact until the year 1888. It then became the property of a café owner who had certain alterations made in the house and converted the ground floor into a billiard room. On one of the walls of the house the municipal authorities had an inscription placed, of which Hill gives the following translation: "Here stood the house in which Antonio Stradivari brought the Violin to its highest perfection and left to Cremona an imperishable name as Master of his craft".

Some twenty-five years ago the house was pulled down entirely and a modern gallery was erected in its place. On one of the columns of this there is a record that the house of Stradivarius once stood there—a peculiar indication indeed, for the column is no thicker than the well which once stood in the courtyard of Stradivarius' house! Thus has Cremona honoured the man to whom the city owes its universal fame. Here, if anywhere, is an example of the saying that "a prophet is not without honour, but in his own country".

A great deal, however, was subsequently done to compensate for this neglect. Not only did the Corporation name one of the principal streets of the city after Stradivarius, but also, in 1930, they devoted a whole room in the Museo Civico to the memory of this artist of genius. There will be found here, for example, a large number of his violin patterns and designs for the various parts of his instruments. Of his tools, unfortunately, only a gauge for measuring the

54

ORNAMENTAL DESIGNS BY STRADIVARIUS

thickness of the soundboard and back has been preserved (see p. 49).
Bergonzi, who as we know took over Stradivarius' workshop, probably used and wore out most of the planes, chisels, knives, files
and saws. Count Cozio di Salabue, who later acquired what was
left of Stradivarius' estate, speaks about tools in his correspondence
with Stradivarius' heirs, but these can no longer be traced. Vuillaume
also secured a few pieces from Stradivarius' workshop, including
various violin patterns, for instance, which he later presented to the
museum of the Paris Conservatoire.

From the large number of patterns preserved in the Museum at
Cremona it would appear that Stradivarius prepared a separate
pattern for every new model that he made, however slight the differences from earlier models may have been. Even for the sound-
holes he made many designs, as is proved by numerous drawings.
The countless designs for bridges, string-holders and pegs for his
various instruments witness to the extreme care Stradivarius devoted
to the making of every component part, however small. He left
nothing to chance and he even made a number of designs for the
locks of the violin cases he made. From various designs for nuts

55

and points it would appear that Stradivarius also made bows for his violins. Although not complete, this collection certainly presents an interesting picture of Stradivarius' methods of work.

As we have already seen, his tombstone and the well from his house are also in this Museum.

In 1937 the City of Cremona commemorated in worthy manner the bicentenary of Stradivarius' death; among other things, a Museum and a school of violin-making were founded and an exhibition of old Cremonese string instruments was held in the Palazzo Cittanova.

It was Stradivarius, of course, who was most generously represented. From a few violoncellos and some fifty violins one could follow step by step the entire development of Stradivarius' art from the year 1667 onwards.

There was, alas, only a single instrument by Stradivarius' sons, a violin made by Omobono in the year 1740 (see p. 43). Stradivarius' pupil Carlo Bergonzi was also only represented by one violin, dating from 1737 (see p. 45).

There was also a choice collection of violins produced by the various members of the Amati family, including an extremely rare specimen by Andreas Amati of the year 1574, one of the 24 instruments which he made for King Charles IX of France (see p. 7). Nicolas Amati was also well represented, for his development could be followed closely from 1653 to 1676. For the sake of completeness there were also instruments by a number of his pupils, such as Giovanni Battista Rogeri and Francesco Ruggeri.

An exceedingly important section was formed by a collection of instruments made by various members of the Guarnerius family. Besides those of Andreas, the founder, there were instruments by his sons Peter and Joseph Guarnerius, but the chief attraction of this exhibit was undoubtedly the unique collection of violins by Joseph Guarnerius del Gesù, a son of the violin maker Gian Battista Guarnerius and Angiola Maria Locadelli, and justifiably, for he was not only the greatest master of that family but also one of the greatest violin makers of all time and in many respects Stradivarius' compeer. He was born in 1687, so that he was some forty years younger than Stradivarius. Many have tried to make out that he was a pupil of Stradivarius, but there is no evidence for this. As we know, both Hill and Hart believe that Joseph was a pupil of his uncle Joseph, the son of Andreas.

56

About his life practically everything is still obscure. What we are continually reading about him, namely, that he spent many years in prison, must be dismissed as legend. This tale probably originated in the fact that in the early part of the 18th century there was indeed a criminal named Guarnerius who landed in prison; his name, however, was not Joseph but Giacomo. Some of the violins of Joseph's last period, hastily and carelessly finished, have been related to this story, being dubbed 'prison violins'.

Guarnerius went his own way absolutely independently of any influence whatsoever. The nickname 'del Gesù' he owes to his

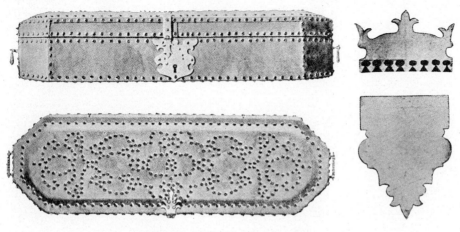

VIOLIN CASE BY STRADIVARIUS

having used on his labels the sacred letters I. H. S., which are a Greek abbreviation of the name of Jesus.

This exhibition offered a unique opportunity of studying the whole development of Guarnerius. It also demonstrated how different from each other the personalities of Stradivarius and Guarnerius were. In Stradivarius we see great uniformity, aristocratic refinement, and evidence of a deeply reflective, searching genius; in Guarnerius, on the other hand, extreme inequality and carelessness to the point of coarseness, but in all his instruments we see manifesting themselves, as it were, the boldness and impetuosity of his genius. The choice of wood, to mention but a single detail, is characteristic. With Stradivarius we find as a rule an extremely fine grain, while with Guarnerius the wood is broader and bolder in texture. In the backward curve of Guarnerius' scrolls there is a vigour, a recurring

VIOLIN BY JOSEPH GUARNERIUS DEL GESÙ, 1742
Paganini's "Cannon"

58

audacity, great determination. Stradivarius' scroll, on the other hand, always charms by its light elegance, lofty grace of line and noble balance and repose.

One of the greatest attractions of the exhibition was undoubtedly Joseph Guarnerius' violin of 1742 with which Paganini conquered the whole of Europe in his triumphal progress. When in 1801 Paganini had to give a concert at Leghorn the merchant Livron lent him this violin. Livron was so enraptured by his playing that after the concert he spontaneously presented the instrument to him. Right up till his death in 1840 Paganini preferred to play on this instrument, which he called his "Cannon" on account of its particularly powerful tone. In his will he bequeathed this violin to his native city of Genoa, where it is kept in a glass case in one of the rooms of the Town Hall.

This violin is undoubtedly one of Guarnerius' most characteristic products—a real Guarnerius, with all his careless and slovenly genius. That Guarnerius was capable, however, of work at least as careful and accurate as that of Stradivarius is proved by the so-called Pugnani violin of 1733 which was included in the exhibition, an instrument which is in no way inferior to a Stradivarius.

But although Guarnerius occasionally made equally fine violins, our Stradivarius nevertheless remains a unique figure in the history of violin making because it was he, after all, who created the instrument of the future.

BIBLIOGRAPHY

Hill (W. Henry), Arthur F. Hill and Alfred E. Hill, *Antonio Stradivari. His Life and Work* (1644–1737). London, 1902.

The *"Salabue Stradivari"*. A history and critical description of the famous violin commònly called "Le Messie". Containing many particulars obtained from authentic sources and now published for the first time. Illustrated with three coloured plates by Mr. Shirley Slocombe. London, 1891.

The *"Tuscan"*. A short account of a Violin by Stradivari made for Cosimo de Medici, Grand Duke of Tuscany, dated 1690. W. E. Hill and Son, London, 1891.

The *"Emperor Stradivari"*. Date 1715. A history and description of the famous violin in the possession of George Haddock. Illustrated with three views. London, 1893.

Hart (George), *The Violin: its famous makers and their imitators.* London, 1875.

Lütgendorff (Willibald Leo Freiherrn v.), *Die Geigen- und Lautenmacher vom Mittelalter bis zur Gegenwart.* Nach den besten Quellen bearbeitet. Frankfurt a. Main, 1912.

Apian-Bennewitz (Paul Otto), *Die Geige, der Geigenbau und die Bogenverfertigung.* Mit einem Atlas. Weimar, 1892.

Spohr (Louis), *Selbstbiographie.* Cassel, 1860-1.

Meyer (Fritz), *Berühmte Geige und ihre Schicksale.* Köln, 1920.

Bacchetta (Renzo), *Stradivari.* Cremona, 1937.

L'Esposizione di liuteria antica a Cremona nel 1937.